# Pouring Echoes

*By n.J.bellacicco*

Copyright © 2017
Tribute Publishing, LLC
Frisco, Texas

Tribute Publishing, LLC

Pouring Echoes
First Edition December 2017

All Worldwide Rights Reserved
ISBN: 978-0-9982860-3-7

All Rights Reserved. No part of this book may be reproduced, stored in a retrieval system, or transmitted, in any form, or by any means, electronic, recorded, photocopied, or otherwise, without the prior written permission of the copyright owner, except by a reviewer who may quote brief passages in a review.

# Introduction

Empathy is everything. It is a gift, but also an acquired ability. It is what I have been after and what I will continue to pursue for the rest of my life. Being vulnerable opens the gateway for compassion. My mission in this book was to be raw. To bottle up experiences and send them out into the unknown ocean, hoping that my bottle will be found and that someone out there does get it.

For the past twenty-two years, I have shouted out to the world and have listened for a reply. Through this process, I have discovered beauty within the misery, joy within the progress, and the awesomeness that is love and human connection. I know that through poetry we can see the world a little clearer.

I wrote this book with one intention: to zoom in and out on the theme of relationships between people. It is about pouring yourself into the family that is our world. The poems are not in chronological order. Rather, after completing the work, I went back and assembled a timeline of my journey. Each poem is placed to allow you, the reader, to join me in discovering what really matters in this life. Some of these poems relate to my life, others to my friends' lives, and others are stories I created to try to understand the pain people are going through every day.

The first chapter is titled →. The forward arrow represents all the moments of shouting out to the world. Whether it be in joy, frustration, or sadness. It is about questioning in order to discover. It is about those nights where you stare up at the sky asking, "Why?" This chapter is about sending out the echo. The second chapter ← is all about listening, understanding, and growth. The backward arrow represents receiving the echo. It is about empathizing with the people in our lives. The final chapter • focuses on siphoning out that truth. It involves acceptance and a new approach to life.

The way in which I ordered these poems is meant to allow you to follow this echo. To empathize with these moments of vulnerability. Each poem emits a sound that I hope allows you to better understand yourself and your calling to connect with those around you. I pray that each poem reminds you that you are not alone on this journey. Enjoy my friends.

It is time.

All the best,

n.J.bellacicco

To Seth Jones.

My friend, thank you for listening.

# Table of Contents

→

agent of change.///3
i think.///4
paddles.///5
paralyzed action.///6
hollow.///7
enter.///9
what do you see.///10
lacerations.///11
for all to see.///12
helium and boulders.///13
coffee.///15
shredded wind.///16
the bus.///17
poem #1.///18
the other side of the moon.///19
be ready.///20
walk forward.///21
curve.///22
rhythm.///23
elation.///24
to fill the earth.///25
anxiety is.///26
adhdadhdadhd.///27
wounded.///28

untitled.///29
not planted.///30
forge.///31
gender tears.///32
let them fall.///33
sacrificed for me.///34
following You.///35
a drop of my blood.///36
tiny lies.///38
am i enough.///39
ember.///40
free falling.///41
intuition.///43
a bubble.///44
bolt.///45
covering.///46
s l o w n e s s.///47
afraid.///48
stressed.///49
treadmill moments.///50
sword lava.///51
fins.///52
scoop.///53
not me.///54
be johnny appleseed.///55
from myself.///56

to all people.///61
confessions of a dining hall worker.///62
the life of screams.///63
my war.///64
in the jail.///65
camp ohana.///66
a flying pen.///68
milliseconds.///69
because of that drop.///70
you must not.///71
blocked lungs.///72
safe house.///73
manhood.///74
indifferent.///75
as we get older.///76
tongues that pillage.///77
parrots.///78
tight.///79
crescent.///80
going.///81
when those you love are hurting.///82
broken puddles.///83
to be close.///85
the silence between prayers.///86
laced to the ground.///87
two packs of tissues.///89
clawed.///90

gold rush.///91
long distance friends.///92
untapped potential.///93
slippers.///94
tattoo.///95
a whisper.///96
she makes me feel.///97
butterfly to caterpillar.///98
blinded.///99
with you i forget.///100
first felt.///101
algae.///102
still glow.///104
loyal friends.///105
steps of ours.///106
flushed.///107
dear dad.///109
to my mother.///110
swing forward.///111
cottoned.///112
to her, him, and him.///113
that is love.///114
my first day of medical school.///115
identity.///116
renewal.///117

●

you know the answer.///121
f.o.c.u.s.///122
your instrument.///123
be the sphere.///124
to be still.///125
the door.///126
ridges.///127
our world.///128
in my fist.///129
venture.///130
rise.///131
not here but here.///132
our Dove.///133
"walk with Me."///134
no bookmarks.///135
ride with me.///136
become.///137
before my eyes.///138
don't run in the rain.///139
on august 16th.///140
clarity.///141
00:00.///142
growth.///144
orion's fingertips.///145
rescind me.///146
prayer.///147
bound.///148

one another.///149
it does not matter.///150
pouring echoes.///151
yes, it is.///152
wheels don't step.///153
machine world.///155
ten.///156
the weight of it all.///157
the pace.///159
x-ray vision.///160
marked up.///161
thanks to give.///162
carry.///163
linked.///164
empathy is the answer.///165
be broken.///166
i will hold up your head.///167
zipper in your chest.///169
sought.///170
infinite…///171
you are not the driver.///172
peace and the cross.///173
write///174

About the Author///176

## agent of change.

Sometimes I strike at the pebbles under my toes
to remind myself that I am capable of
setting the earth into motion.

## i think.

If I know what I have to do
Why do I question my knowing?

If I know what I need to do
Why do I seek an answer?

If I know what I must do,
Why do I not begin?

A life born of whys stops
the restless dawn.

# paddles.

I don't know why,
But
Some days I feel like a canoe
absorbed into a lazy lake,
sloshing around waiting for
anyone to notice my unchartered
movement.

The paddles jut out
like daggers that could very well
pierce into the water's
flesh.

But I sit still. Afraid to touch
the wooden weapons. As if I
am incapable. A carpenter afraid
of the saw passed down from his father.

My paddles fell in the water.
It is far too late. The wood has become
stone. The flesh has drowned them.


Most days, I want to be a sailor.
Waiting for someone to tell me,
it is okay to take hold of the paddles.

## paralyzed action.

Lord, help me see beyond
the floorboards.
Place me in the center of
the blooming rose.
Sweep the fog from
my lashes.
Dissolve the dirt from
my tongue.

Lord, they are paralyzed.
Because I can't see them
cry while underwater.

# hollow.

We bore the box from the hutch.
Ceremony commenced with a dig—
a crunch to hollow the earth.
Hollow—just as the maggots did to her.

6 foot, 220 pounds
Yet his tears tore him down—
my little brother's sturdy frame.
I wished to carry him in the palm of my heart.
Yet, how could I understand?
He, the guardian, scrutinized as
the clawed coffin kissed dirt.

A movement, convulsion, spread from
the welded walls.
A sharp squeal bent the cosmos—
a ripple turned our picket fence to shards.

She, the hare, eaten alive. Inside to out.
The shrills ate at my brother.
Bit by bit.
He cried, "There were too many—
I couldn't rip them from her."

She pounded the grass.
Again. And Again.
Wanting to find her final burrow.

The solid side of the shovel gleamed.

A sheet steel sword sat at my toes.
It would only—
take a second.

The shovel was at my toes.
Paralyzed, by her seizures.

The shovel was at my toes.
But, my brother.

The shovel was at my knees.

But my brother.

**enter.**

Is an exit
not but an
entrance
to an untouched
possibility?

## what do you see.

Will there ever be a day.
When I look at my neighbor.
And see the good before the bad?

Will there ever be a day
When I look at my neighbor,
And see the good before the bad?

## lacerations.

Every person I know is a piece of the dam
Holding me back
from draining out of life's lacerations.
I only hope that one day my pool runs dry.
And I can come to your aid.

## for all to see.

I want to put my emotion on a plate.
Out on the dinner table, for all to see.
I want emotion so raw that when I put
him out on the dinner table to be served,
he will shout at me because he is alive
and he knows he is naked.

## helium and boulders.

I call her Helium.
Though, she doesn't know it.
Abundant in the atmosphere.
Yet, she's so rare here.
On earth.
But I found her.

She's rather uplifting.
Gosh. With her I'm
lighter than air.
I float now, on
our noble throne.

Unlike Helium, you are
not #2 at my table.
Unlike Helium, you are
a gust
of powdered rainbow.

Now, the Boulders, well, they
remain.
"Crawl beneath
and dig me up."
They call.
All the while,
they press down.

At a time, I hoped the Boulders
were hollow. But
now I know, rocks only levitate
when tornados come.

Don't seep
from
my rubbered skin.
I'm falling.
Breathe   into   me.

I call her Helium.
Though, she doesn't know it.

## coffee.

If I'm being honest
You remind me of
lukewarm coffee.

Well, our relationship does.
What we have is no longer—

burn-your-tongue-
at-first-taste hot.
Not touch-a-black-limo-in-
a-desert hot.

Nor is it tongue-stuck-to-
pole cold.
Nor is it snow-covered-hands-
no-pockets cold.

Lukewarm.

Yet, somehow when filled up by your presence.
You still continue to energize me.

## shredded wind.

With you, I am strung to the face
of a train. Flowing like water through
hot pipes pressed towards you.

The end of the tunnel echoes the light.
Throughout the way the speed
shreds the wind, slices sound, and breaks my
words into syllables. My pupils are shattered
into pieces of memories.

Once I make it to the end of the tracks,
I am a battered man.
My clothes liquid cotton: frail, and worn.
The wind shredded at my skin but you
washed my wounds.
And then brought me home.

## the bus.

The bus started.
He turned to her and said,
"I'll see you soon."
The General tapped his foot.

She held his hand.
Her thumb fell on his right index finger.
Would his be quicker to press the trigger
than the finger of those waiting to take him
away?

"Love you—be safe," she said.
She wanted to believe, with all her being,
that her words alone could stop a bullet.
Could make his finger quicker.

## poem #1.

Lately, I've been shattered.
Searching for the pieces of my frailty.
The light of the world is cigarettes
trying to put itself out by scarring me.

Then you came.

Like a bricklayer,
unafraid to put me back in place.
Building a castle around us,
so that nothing could crack me again.

I'm holding the deck.
When the cards fall all I see
are 4, 2, 9, of hearts. Always.

I understand why the wolves howl at night.
They long for their other half, lost,
scattered in the forest.

Lately, I've felt more than I thought I could feel.
My lightning pains have melted to sunsets.

## the other side of the moon.

You are not my other half
but my best half.
There is a difference.

The earth rotates but we only get to see
one half of the moon.
I was the covered, hidden.
Unaware that my other side
had so much light to give.

## be ready.

She met me under the library light
I lost the script of who I was to be
We met beneath the covering of night
My voice, nailed like a sign on a tree

The more she spoke, the more I had forgot
How much I cared; to hide from pain of loss.
The rainclouds flew and my few words were caught.
Her eyes dance off mine, dream to cross.

Her chair left below skids like broken snow
My legs as weighty as metallic beams
She walks away, behind she leaves her glow.
Stranded wading in the cruel frozen streams

At once, like Zechariah, I did speak
"A future not tried, is a future bleak."

## walk forward.

Vibrant vibration I hear in my vicinity
Her voice echoes, encircling my mind
Like a swarm of bees engulfing a lily
She is my flower, my later on
Sweet smile stills the dawn

Yet, here I stand wilting
Waiting to send a sound wave her way
Each wading minute a petal is unstrung from my core
*Now it is time! Hold on, stop, be sure*
Petals persistently plummeting, longing is eager.

It is a curse to ponder.

The last of the leaves drop
She is effaced from my timeline
If a word had been sent, would she have been?
Will I ever broadcast vibrant vibrations into my vicinity?
If not, in these moments I lose our infinity.

**curve.**

When I hug you
  even your spine
    pushes itself
        away
    from
me.

## rhythm.

If a stethoscope can understand the nature of
your heart,
Why can't I?

## elation.

the wind lifts my toes
the clouds slip between my eyelashes
the rain waters my rocking heart
and grows a healing fire in my spine.


Elevation.


I cannot remember where it hurt
because pain is now a mystery
The Artist painted over my cracks with
molten joy and flowing peace.

## to fill the earth.

For she was convinced
that the earth was hollow.
And tried to fill it with her wrist blood.
Each sawing of her veins,
a bucket poured into the core.

For the knife was a friend
Reminding her that the world was empty.
The only way to fill it, was to leave it behind.
Take your limbs and pour them like concrete
into the abyss.

Her breath weighted hummingbirds.
Eyes drawn towards
the scarlet stains on her bedspread.
The earth was consuming her,
siphoning life from her fluttering heartbeat.

She took a bandage and wrapped it
again and again.
The blood dissolved into the white linen
forming an image. Of the world.
Overflowing with her tears.

## anxiety is.

I am sitting in a catapult.
Waiting for the world
to pull the trigger.
And maybe mother earth won't.
But she has the ability.
And in the ability comes the fear.

## adhdadhdadhd.

The microscopic squirrel nibbles on my spine.
He weaves through my legs. I must shake him out!

The curl on my friend's lip is peculiar when she smiles.
I need to get out of this classroom. Now.
When I run I am free.
Sitting = Chinese water torture + tickled by a feather on my pinky toe.

I like her a lot. How long have I been staring?
This squirrel won't leave me alone.
I want to take a BB gun to its skull.
But it has become an old friend now.
Without it, am I really me?

**wounded.**

I put a tourniquet around my chest
to stop the bleeding.
But now my heart
            is dead.

**untitled.**

He walked into the house
and did not realize the lights were off.
That is when he knew he needed help.

## not planted.

I don't know what it means to be rooted anymore.

How can I stay?
Everywhere is in need of change.

Can I be that difference?

I don't want to be a potted plant.
But pollen.
With a blueprint itching beneath my skin.

I don't want to be rooted.

## forge.

The more often I sign
my name, the more I feel
my identity escape.

Sometimes, I sign with my
left hand to surprise myself.
To uncover a new part of me.

## gender tears.

When a man cries the world
Stops.
When a woman cries the world
Spins.
I do not understand.
Why do we assign our tears genders?

**let them fall.**

Every time I cry
someone knocks on my bedroom door.

Bring the day where my tears can fall freely
Without the fear that they will land
in stranger's palms.

## sacrificed for me.

for they took everything away from you
and that made you worry
not for yourself, but for me
teach me how to live that way?
to forget myself.

i want to be the world's provider
but my arms have been glued to my own body
and my eyes cemented to the mirror.

## following You.

Help me go where I am supposed to go
Be where I am supposed to be
Love where I am supposed to love.
Let me be like a river waterfall,
sending droplets among the outer banks
to the flowers not yet born.
Let it be in my nature
To pour myself into You.

## a drop of my blood.

My friend tiptoes up to the glass fortress.
His hands slide against the shark tank.
The great whites crave his fingerprints.

"What are you doing?" I shout.

He doesn't turn around. He never has.
His fingers poke through the famished glass.
His body dissolves through the glass.
Eyes buried in the murk of marine water.

"Why are you doing this?" I yell.

Three sharks circle above him.
Monkshood flowers sprout from the three
undersides, emitting a drenched purple.

He can't hear my punches. He doesn't notice
the blood leak from my knuckles.
The sharks sprinkle the floral poison.
A wedding ceremony commences between
my friend and his tempters.

"Come back to me," I cry.

The glass fractures from the weight of my
blood.

I shiver as I trace the uncharted lines.
A drop of my blood mixes with his water.

Gasping for air, my friend reaches for me.
The sharks, now three minnows, crushed
between his fingers. The flowers droop from
their tongues.

"They are gone," I say.
Together, we unlock his frozen grip on the
flowered minnows.
With both hands he swims for the surface.

**tiny lies.**

I tell her that everything is going to
be okay.
That was the biggest lie I've ever whispered to
her.

Last year I said, "I love you"
That was a small lie, yet
I didn't understand the perpetual damage.

## am i enough.

"I'll never be enough."
she thought as she gripped the steering wheel.
sitting at the red light.
she had her foot pressed on the brake.
she was not going anywhere.

her younger brother spoke up
from the back seat
and he talked about
his toy car collection and
his favorite soccer players
he knew she would listen
and she did
and answered back
and that was
enough
for him to smile.

she eased off her brake
she noticed the green light.

**ember.**

I'm a burnt piece of wood
trying to be a tree again.

# free falling.

My lungs are being pulled
Like tug of war.
My body wrapped with sheets made of boa skin.
I want to get out of bed but I'm afraid
If I do, I'll never find rest again.

I want to cover my walking body with pillows.
But I know when I do,
they will turn to bird excretions.
Weighing me down,
unable to scrape off my limbs.

Bridges scare me because how
can something so thin not break?
It makes me question my own ability to
crumble.
It's a thin line you know?
The line between being nervous
and having your body
Tell you that death is a heartbeat away.

When I was a kid I used to walk on the curb.
If I fell off, the sharks would eat me alive.
It's funny how childhood shapes you.
Becoming bait was my reality.

Sometimes life unhooks me.
When I sit in the pew.
When she kisses me.
When I listen to the laughter of my brothers.
When I hug my grandma.
I am free to fall.

**intuition.**

I'll never know when to believe you
and to not believe myself.

## a bubble.

I awaken on the 50th floor
of stone. My hands press on the outer wall
of the building. There is no windows, small
cracks, or even ledges to grasp. To hold the
weight of myself.

My palms pour and the liquid flows through the
lines spider webbing across my hand.

I start to slip.

The walls are now covered in dish soap
and summer rain.
The downward fall and the pressing of my
hands causes bubbles to form. To build up.

I still slip.

I'm on the 3rd floor now. The more I fight, the
more I fall, the more bubbles I make.

Then I hit.

The bubbles that formed become
a pillow to my feet.
They absorbed me and I leave the ground.
Floating up.
To the 51$^{st}$ floor.

## bolt.

I wish to
touch the cool
and misty
lightning bolt.
Allow the energy to
burrow into each nerve.
Radiate my weak and brittle bones.
Rattle and break with frustrated electrocution
the shackles of resignation.

**covering.**

If I covered my mouth instead of my heart.
Maybe, you would understand.

## s l o w n e s s.

Turtles are slow, but have a shell,
to block them from the savage of time
I seek an unhurried life, a life of contemplation
As my skin ages, it softens.
I become a slug, holding onto the last rock,
gravity peels me away

My only hope, is that I can leave a trail,
along the cobblestone streets.

## afraid.

Why do we make our creeks
oceans?
Why do we turn our bickering
into war?
Why do we morph our need for more
into poverty?

For we are fearful of ourselves.
Cast away by our own shadowed glance.
Untrusting of our right and left feet.

When we speak even our tongues
hit us in reprimand.

**stressed.**

the funny thing about being stress free.
is that it is free.

## treadmill moments.

I'm running on a treadmill
A treadmill going too fast to do anything
but run.

Can't stop it.
Can't jump off.
I can just run.
As fast as I can.

I want to get off.
But the more I think about it
my knees buckle.
So I focus on the running.

Then there will be a time when I run too fast.
The machine will overheat.
My sneakers melting like a summer ice pop.
I will stop.
I will look around.
And see that I am sitting on my bed.
Thinking about my future.

## sword lava.

I am hurting the world.
My inaction, a sword, thrust into the ocean.
Falling like treasure untouched.
Until
    rock
        bottom.

Slices ocean floor.
Inadequacy flaunts inaction.
Sword buried under the cover of shells.
Earth's marrow, lava, bleeds from the gash.

The sword metal does not melt
It becomes a deep brand
Forces itself against the ocean floor

In due time, we all make the choice.
To act or omit
To live or believe we are alive.

## fins.

My fish has a problem.
He floats on his side
and tries to stay upright.
At times, his marine head cuts against
the algae stained gravel.
He can't find the surface.

I think his fins work fine.

He is not hungry.
Why is he sick?
What am I to do?
I can't repair him.

He flips upside down
and then right side up.
At times, his fins tap the glass,
calling for me to help.

I think his fins work fine.

He is not hungry.
Why is he sick?
I want to do something.
Anything to ease his suffering.
How do I help when I can never swim in his water?

## scoop.

How can something so fake seem so real?
Why were we made this way?
To feel so deeply.
Only being able to scoop the water from the pool with the spoon we have been given.

## not me.

I've been waiting for your call.
I know you know that I am.

Have you ever been to a restaurant where
they hand you a little buzzer?
The one that seizes
when they have a table for you?
That is how it feels.
What you are doing to me.
May I join the table?

So, I decide to walk into the restaurant
without the buzz
Without the sound of my welcome.
Only to find out, you already finished your meal.

## be johnny appleseed.

I hate it when people throw apple cores in the trash.
Each seed has potential and yet you just
drop it into a barren black hole? Lost. Gone.

Whenever I eat an apple, I hide it.
I drop it in a bush.
Dig a hole so small the seed melts in the dirt.
We must give each offspring a chance.

We are quick to get rid of opportunity
once we eat our fruit.
Why do we not cultivate?

## from myself.

I'm waiting for the day
my shaking hands start a fire.

That turns to ash
the breathless vines of insecurity.

I'm waiting for the day
my tears build a river.

That drowns the doubts
which float to the surface.

I'm waiting for the day
my screams hit the stars.

That ignites them
for all to see.

I'm waiting for the day
Where I hold the key to my body
And can free myself
from myself.

## to all people.

I'll never know that you were sad.
And that makes me sad.

## confessions of a dining hall worker.

"Hi, how are you doing?"
*Swipe.*
"Hi, how are you doing?"
*Swipe.*
"Hi, how are you doing?"
*Swipe.*
"Hi, how are you doing?"
*Swipe.*
"Hi, how are you doing?"
"I'm doing great today, how is your husband doing?"

*Swipe.*

## the life of screams.

Everyday I walk by thousands of screams.
Locked behind the teeth of strangers.

Screams of poverty, illness, and sorrow.
Of failure and lost loves.

Sometimes the screams slip out as
"Get lost."
or
"I hate you."
or
"I don't care."

I must then remind myself that screams like disguise.

And what I really hear is,
"Don't ever leave me."

**my war.**

I just want you to know
the battle you are facing
is also my war.
When you trudge through the mud
my combat boots get dirty.
When you anticipate the enemy
my ears are listening.
When you get shot
my chest carries the bullet.

# in the jail.

We sit in the jail cell
key in our hands.
Escape is slivers of air away.

We push the key in the slot
It will not fit.
We see that it is backwards in hand.
It cannot be turned because it is
cemented to our very fingers.

Escape was just slivers of air away.
It becomes even more difficult when
we see the way but are helpless.

until we realize the door was always open
we didn't even need a key

and we were not in a cell
but a safe place

where we hid
in order to learn how to move forward

## camp ohana.

We slipped each foot into the masked ocean.
Our scuba gear secure. Safe.
We had one common goal.
*Reach the other side of the deep blue water.*

We readied ourselves for the dive.
We saw the sharp fin sticking out of the murky maze.
We knew all it would take was a single touch and we would never make it to the other side.

Our feet pushed against the fizz and bubbles.
Each stroke, possibly our last.
One of our fellow minnows gobbled up.
Lost.
Just like that.

But. There was no turning back.

Reach the other side. *Reach the other side. Reach the other*—we bellowed together like whale conversation.
Another. Touched by the teeth of the shark.
Another. Gone yet unseen.
Like gills sifting through sea.

But. There was no turning back.

I must have been sweating when I reached the
other side.
I must have—but the water swallowed each
bead up.
Just like those in my school.

I ripped off my gear and dipped my safe face
into the waves.  I heard a buoyant voice,
"Lunch is ready," said grandma
"Time to dry off."

## a flying pen.

When he had a day off he would go
to the airport.
Take off his boots.
Go through the portal.
And write.

The people were his stories.
Their clothes his script.
Smiles and angered brows
set the tone for the feature film.

When he had a day off he would go
to the airport.
Not to fly, but to soar into the unknown
timelines of the journeymen.

## milliseconds.

I can begin at any instant.
Is that not the most incredible thing?
Each day I unshroud my lids and awaken.
I can become an utterly different man
in
milliseconds.

I think I stay the same but
my cells continue to shout
different dialogues as they
die and are reborn. These are changes
where I don't hold the reigns.

Sometimes, I feel like
the traffic lights under my shoes
emit green and red at the same time.

At least it is not yellow, I remind myself.

## because of that drop.

Some days caring for the world
Feels like I have a bucket brimming with water.
A daisy ten miles out into the desert.

I carry my bucket.
When I reach the flower
all that is left is a single drop.

Because of that drop.

I go back, and do it again.

## you must not.

Go back.

Your mind is a rolling hill
and your thoughts are boulders.
Behind you sits a meadow with a
glass of water. A table with an empty seat.

Go back.

At the top of the mountain sits a glass jar
filled with unquestioned laughter and love that is
effortless.

Go back.

The rocks will never stop.
Maybe, it would be easier to listen
to the sound of the crushed grass.
Subject to the weight of the stones.

Go back.

Go back, you cannot.
Because even when you look back.
You can hear the glass jar rattle.
That is enough.

## blocked lungs.

You bring your face into my breastplate
Each huff and wail harmonized with a
tighter pull of my three day, hospital-scented,
white undershirt. You want to merge with me
because you think I am the stronger
half in our brotherhood.
Your tears burn a hole in the cloth,
burrow into my skin, and use my lungs as a
resting place.

That tear and all his friends clog me.
I can no longer say,
"Mom fought for a long time."
Because I fear if I open my mouth and
let the breath escape, I will lose the
last drip of my strength.

## safe house.

Like a chair,
It is my duty to hold the weight of you.
Without me, how can you rest your feet?
Like a chair, I strive to bring stability.
I am a four-pillared safe house.

Like a chair, I am always where you left me
Awaiting your return home
However, like a chair, I may break
After years of taking on the weight
I can crumble.

Remember this
I am a chair, your chair
Always here to hold you
Always a safe house
Yet, weight is still weight

Though distinct, we are all made from the same material.

## manhood.

To be a man you must drink
Water to stay alive, but a whole lot of beer.

To be a man you must never cry
Tears are inexcusable.

To be a man you must kill things
Like deer, and rabbits, and your humility.

To be a man you must raise a child
and your standards
Because unattractive women won't raise you up.

To be a man you have to display courage
and walk along the beach with bulging muscles.

To be a man you must always win.
At life.
At sports.

To be a man you must never die.

To be a man, you must be alone.

**indifferent.**

He's the type of man that would see a
Cheerio on the kitchen floor.
Crush it under his boot.
And walk away.

Spreading his destruction wherever he walked.
Don't be like that man.

## as we get older.

We don't need to stop talking.

We must stop mimicking.

Because we are the example now.

## tongues that pillage.

If I took 365 days of talk
Sealed the words in a jar
Would I have a treasure chest?
Or a bomb?
That has already gone off.

## parrots.

They call her parrot.
"No ideas of her own,"
They say.

I thought she was quite
unique. Beautiful in every
feather that she owned.

They say,
"She is not novel.
She quotes the voices of others.
She does not form her own opinion."

"Interesting." I say.
"Yes." They say in unison.

## tight.

You are a tie around my neck.
With you I look good, sharp, classy.
I am professional.

Yet, the closer you pull towards me,
the tighter the noose becomes
around my neck.

## crescent.

She drops her iPhone into a pond
of tears.
All the photos of them
evaporate in formless air.

The wedding band whittles itself through the counter.
She tries to grab it, but the empty hole in the middle weighs three tons.

No note. No explanation.

Half the closet, now a black hole
The other a crescent flowered earth.
The empty.
Just as the grenades that flew from her mouth.
Each explosion, further glides the ring off his tear-coated finger.

## going.

Her phone buzzed on the subway.
The entire 21-minute ride.
Uptown to Downtown.
She never once shut it off.
Just looked down. Stared at his
name with a heart etched into the digital world.

She wanted to know
how much he cared that she had left him.
She needed to know
that her departure hacked at his heart.
*BUZZ.*

Each vibration to her a victory.
To him each buzz a vicious earthquake
reshaping his fused ground.

## when those you love are hurting.

When those you love are hurting
You forget about your pain
The bruises of their day
beneath you wax and wane.

When those you love are hurting
You try your best not to cry
The pressure they are under
has you asking *why*.

When those you love are hurting
You become frozen in fear
Because the monster they are against
becomes the voice you always hear.

## broken puddles.

Children jump into puddles
after it rains because they
feel the need to press down against
the vulnerable water. Crack its shell and walk
away.


Is this how you feel when you hit me?


In our house it rains.
The water runs down the steps.
The drops spring off the
pots and the kettle. Sizzle on the stove.

The rainwater rushes in one direction
like an overflowing canopy leaf in a rainforest.
I lay on the jungle floor because I'm in
quicksand.
I float, if not, I will drown.

The water drips off the leaf and pools into the
recesses of my closed eyes.
I hear you walk close to me.
I know you see the puddles and by instinct
plummet your fist into each tiny lake.

The once clear water blends to a tender purple.
We don't talk about it now, because the rain has stopped.
There are no puddles for you anymore—
for now.
But, when the wind picks up, I quiver.

Will you ever understand?
I am more than a few puddles.
I am the ocean.
And the ocean always outlasts the storm.

## to be close.

He stood outside the bathroom door.
His head resting on the door frame.
Trying to rip off the cemented doorknob.
Whispering over the sounds he hated to hear.

"I'm here. You don't need to do this."
But it continued. And he stayed.
She came out.
Eyes a ruptured red.
Wiping the spit from her lips.

He kissed her anyway,
It was the only way he could taste her pain.

## the silence between prayers.

Between prayers the dew fell from the lilies.
Like the tear which glides down the cheek
of the child's mother.

Between prayers the cancer ignited
Fireworks buried in his budding torso.

Between prayers there was a silence

A silence built with hope and spackle
Molded by nervous tremors and bouts of rage.

## laced to the ground.

She clung to the sandy grass dunes and
tugged at the blades to escape.
The skunk scent was sewn into her clothes.

Laced.

A woman a few years older yet identical chased
her with a dull ax along the beach.
"Help, Help," the sand covered woman cried
out to the moonlight-tinted ocean.

She slid into the water and grabbed a picket
fence floating in the middle of waves and murk.
The ax woman followed behind in a boat.

With scarred arms the younger woman dove
under.
She had lost the surface. The water nestled its
way into her nose and mouth. Coated her teeth.
That was it.
The women with the ax hit her spine,
made a gash, and climbed inside.

An angel grabbed the young woman
by the shoulders.
He lifted her smothered face from the clawed
hole near the backyard fence.

She tried to speak but instead coughed up pieces of pebbles and roots.
He guided her into the cottage and put a washcloth to her fingernails.
Chaperoned her to bed.

The angel clicked off the lights and took hold of the pen on the dresser. He needed it to finish his spelling homework.

## two packs of tissues.

She carries two little packs of tissues.
One for when she cries.
One for when she laughs.
Whenever she cries she uses that pack
to carry away her tears.
Whenever she laughs, she pulls a tissue
from the pack and pretends to blow her nose.
At the end of the week she compares the two.
This was a good week.

## clawed.

On the weekends, my sister goes on the safari.
With him – the guide.

In the morning she comes back.
Scarred. Bruised. Torn.
"It was the tiger," she replies.

Last time, it was the lion.

I ask, "Why is the guide not hurt?"
She does not answer as I try to bandage her
wounds with white linen.

Bandages glide off her as she goes to the door
The guide always waits outside at midnight.
"But aren't the animals asleep?" I ask.

In the morning she comes back.
Pupils clouded with the terror of the jungle.
Scarred. Bruised. Torn.

I look outside at him.
The guide sits in his white jeep wrangler.
He waves at me, with his worn claws.

**gold rush.**

I'm covered in molten dirt.
You bring out the chisel
and uncover the gold beneath my flesh.

## long distance friends.

The distance between those I love creates wonder.
Wonder, in who they are to me.

When the petal of the wildflower rests over your eye,
You cannot appreciate it.

Only when you see the meadows from a distance.

## untapped potential.

Cheers. He said.
To our past failures and our future successes.
And that is when I realized.
We all have and all will be.

## slippers.

He gave her his slippers
even though the floors were tile.
His feet vulnerable as they
touched down on the icy terrain.

Her toes snug in the fur as she
glided upon the frozen glass.
He gave her his slippers and
that was all she ever wanted.

**tattoo.**

Captured within the locket
Bounded by the clasp


Breathing                quivering
Ferocious                palms

Her image tattooed on my spine
My vision unable, my whole knows

## a whisper.

An angel whispered in my ear last night.
And said why I was given you.

That my fingers were sculpted by God
to melt into yours.
That when we hold one another we are
two broken pieces of vase welded back
together to carry the world.

That your voice was made to flow
through my ear and calm my heart.
That our eyes were made to blink at the
same time in order to never be hidden.

It was only a whisper, but it carried with it
trumpets and the divine Voice.

Together, the angel will never leave.

## she makes me feel.

When she comes near I feel as though raw asphalt emits itself from all my pores. Hardens. Leaves me burning on the inside but unable to break the binding. When she looks at me I feel as though shooting stars are being sent from her iris like an automatic rifle. When she laughs with me I feel as though I could run a marathon. Backwards. On my hands. When she cries I feel as though each of her tears rolls around in my brain like a bowling ball on cocaine. When she is no longer with me, I feel as though the earth's axis has tilted and I am falling.

She makes my feelings become stories.

That is why I can never let her go.

## **butterfly** to caterpillar.

How often we forget that God can mold
two into one.
How the veins on my arms are rivers that
connect with the grey sea of your eyes.
How the flutter of your lashes synchronizes with
my pounding heart. How each leaping sun is a
reminder that I will soon hear the morning song
of your being.

We are separated by canyons and cracks,
trees and train tracks. I can no longer feel our
lungs lift and fall like the tides.

We are butterflies resting in different gardens.
In the garden I continue to pray.
For us to become caterpillars again.
So we may rest in the cocoon together.

## blinded.

If I went blind tomorrow
If all I could see was the night of my eyelids.

I would be okay.

Because I have the memory of you.
And that is all I would choose to see.

## with you i forget.

The two were underwater.
Ink of their lives tattooed on rising bubbles.

Their ocean coated hands connect
Like boats attached to harbor.

To kiss, underwater, was setting sail.
Forgetting that the surface was necessary.

## first felt.

When I look into your eyes
I forget how to breathe.
When I kiss you
I forget how to see.
When I lose you
I forget how to be.

For your touch is my cornerstone.
I do not remember when I first felt summer rain.
But holding you must be the same.

## algae.

The first time I kissed you
is a shattered mirror that I'm
trying to glue back with wet
duct tape. I do this to avoid the mirage
and become "us" again.

Our rowboat tipped over again and I can
no longer carry you to shore.
The clothes you wear are made of paperweights
that hold the script for each
act of our time together.
The boat is taking in the water
and I can only see you
under the murk of the lake.
There is algae thickened upon my brainstem.

I can no longer turn on the record player of
your voice. A sound
lost in the abyss of silence. Silence.
The liquid clock and its gears
churn our memories over and over and over.
Our reality has become an infinite puzzle,
yet always missing a single piece of the past.

But I still dream. I dream to build.
Brick by brick. Slapping on
the cement.

A castle of protection I resurrect around myself.
So, I never am woken up.

## still glow.

I've never been afraid to die.
To drift asleep while the stars still glow.
Until one day I saw the stars in your eyes.
Now I am afraid.
Because if I leave, who will appreciate.

## loyal friends.

Earlobes.
We all have them
They bounce up and down
when we are with joy.
They put their bodies down in
sorrow when we mourn.

Such true friends. If you are lucky,
you have more than one.
Lifelong partners.

Yet, sometimes we decide to pierce them.
Stab them through the torso
and bury them with a diamond.
Studded flower.

**steps of ours.**

The cup of my ancestors is
poured over each step I take

If I walk towards gardens,
the orchids expand in vitality.

If I walk towards the alleys,
the water mourns steam.

## flushed.

For 22 revolutions, I
decided to place a key to my tongue.

Twist it.
Locked.

Then I flushed it down the toilet.

I would trot down the steps to the kitchen.
My parents stared with a genuine zeal for my
existence.

A few words dripped onto my tongue but
they were too big
to fit through the cage bars across my mouth.

"Morning," I said.
A word with so little substance
it oozed through the key hole.
They had opened the doors of their throats
and showered me with words
that I dressed in orange jumpsuits.

I love you. I care. I need you. I want everything
for you. I will always pray for you.

My tongue kicks, ready to lasso the words.
Tear the shackles off the captured angels.
However, I am stopped.
By the clank of the key in the pipe above my head.

**dear dad.**

I went to the kitchen before dawn.
And fixed the coffee for her.
A day commenced with love.
That was when I realized
I am becoming my father.

**to my mother.**

I asked God for guidance.
I prayed for a friend.
I asked God for peace in silence.
I ended my prayer in Amen.

My answer is always before me.
A woman of my own d.n.a.
She smiled and looked towards me.
A thousand thanks I could not say.

Thank you for hugging me
when I was falling apart.
Thank you for carrying me
when my legs did not start.
Thank you for listening
when the world shut its ears.
Thank you for friendship the past 22 years.

## swing forward.

He held the chains that held her up.
"Let go Daddy, I'm ready," she said.
Her dangling feet flying above the
newly dispersed mulch.

Letting go.

To him it was the same as pushing her away.
She would soar back to his arms. And he would
need to let go, again and again, in order for her
to gain momentum.

It would give her the courage to press her
arms past the chains and fly
Landing safely in the prepared footprints.

**cottoned.**

The swallow garnered the cotton
Her young swaddled through action
They would never fall
Because she taught them security

## to her, him, and him.

I'm the big brother.
Sometimes I really live up to the "big" part.

But, I've also been the small brother
and I'm sorry for that.
Because I could have done more.
Spent more time with you.
Hugged you for no reason.
Encouraged, instead of walked away.

When I was younger I did not understand
that losing you is my biggest fear.
Maybe, that is why I hid away?
Because the more I loved you,
the more I feared losing you.

## that is love.

*Thank you*, doesn't suffice.

It never will.

Because while they themselves were crying,
they used both their hands to
wash away my tears.

## my first day of medical school.

When I walked through the doors
I did not think, "I am here."

Because it was not the end.
Nor the beginning.
But a piece of the life-long wandering.
To learn what is necessary.
In order to serve and carry on.

When I walked through the doors.
I did not think, "I am here."
But rather,
I whispered,
"Here I am."

# identity.

"What is your name?" I asked out of instinct.
He stared with his cataract-clothed eyes.
Uncertain and strained.

"I don't know," he said.
Bingo chips rolled between his fingers.
The numbers formed a timeline of his past.

I could never know.
Without a name, could I discover?
Are all his deeds dissolved?

"I don't know," he said again.

The women turned towards me.
"He has trouble – now," she said.
His present state zip-tied his frontal lobe.

"I don't know," he said.
Ashamed. Still he tried.
His forehead burned effort.

"It's okay," she said to him.
She touched his shoulder.
Selfless, he asked me, "What is your name?"

**renewal.**

Today, I wear black.
To mourn the death of my former self.

## you know the answer.

*Be content in all circumstances.*
All?
All.

## f.o.c.u.s.

For if
  Only you
    Could
      Understand the life within each
      Second.

## your instrument.

Life is the saxophone's sound.
Invigorating and sharp, all in one tune.
We lay on the notes, helpless
to the rise and fall,

Until we learn that we clutch
the instrument.
And that the notes we see
we choose to play.

## be the sphere.

be careful
because you are a sphere
infinite, an eternal gift.
The world admires edges.
fine-tuned ideals, rigidity.
boxes stacked like cinderblocks
in a square building.
be careful, do not be compressed.
for spheres roll along the mud
but edges dissolve into the dirt.

## to be still.

In order for a ship to stay firm,
The sailor must lift his loaded anchor
filled with scars,
                dents,
                              and neglect

And drop it into the sea.

In order for our lives to find grounding,
We must let go of our edged rocks
and not carry them any longer.
Watch them fall like soaring doves

 Into the blue

And sit back in weightless security.

## the door.

When you knock
Knock vigorously
Allow your knuckles to form
grooves in the oak.
Switch hands if necessary.
But always have a hand on the knob.
For when the moment is
It will turn.
And the river of red
will be overcome by the radiance
behind the door.

## ridges.

the ridges of the seashell are like us.
smoothed out to perfection
by the breaking tides.

**our world.**

The cup of the world is brimming with
saltwater.
You can't stop drinking from it.

Today, you choose to dump it into the sea.

Sit on shore.
With hands now free.
Folded in prayer.

## in my fist.

i will not let the world take it from me.
i will not allow it.
i have peace nestled within both my clutched
fists.
it is mine to keep.
mine to choose when to let it go.

**venture.**

We adventure for so long
that the world thinks we are dead.

Yet,

we are more alive
than ever before.

**rise.**

You are only given
so many sunrises.
Be with them.
For they are life's joyful delta.

## not here but here.

I didn't want to be here.
I wanted to be there.
But here I am.

I breathe in a day the world has not seen.
Wherever I am, my shoelaces are tied.
Because I know I have somewhere to be.
A place set out for me to move towards.

## our Dove.

the Dove sits at the bottom of my bed
pecking at the sheets until I touch carpet

the Dove sings when I cry
to muffle my quivering limbs

the Dove places His wings on my back
to garnish my flight.

## "walk with Me."

Make
everyday
another step
of thanks.

## no bookmarks.

I live by Day not by days.
At birth Day begins.
At death Day ends.

Why is the sun our bookmark?
Every breath the pages continue to turn.

**ride with me.**

Remember, it is not always an uphill battle.
At times, life is a downhill sleigh ride.
Live for those moments.

**become.**

Fold me into the mountains
So that I may become a diamond.

Pack me in the sea
So that I may become a treasure chest.

Lay me in the snow
So that I may see my halo.

**before my eyes.**

What more can a man ask for
besides the mountains and the sea?

Between both he is pinched between the fingers
of the Creator.
Voyaging along the palm of the Almighty.

## don't run in the rain.

when it rains they told me
don't run, but walk.
if you run they said
you will get more wet.

it does not really make sense

is that not how life is?
when we are getting rained on
we run frantic, afraid.
the light water droplets become
balls of clay sticking to our unaccepting
bodies.

it does not really make sense.

we need to do something different.
walk in the rain.
walk with your chin up, and your feet steady
even though it does not feel right
because sometimes your gut is a liar
and you need to listen to your soul.

## on august 16th.

I do not worry.
Because after every thunderstorm
I have been through
iridescence evolves in the sky.

## clarity.

The person that lifts the cloud
covering your sight is the one.

Not because they uncover.
Because they show you that your
vision has been compromised all along.

It is up to you now, to fight the weather each
morning.

## 00:00.

I find myself on the revolving face of the watch.
With her.

At the hour hand, we sit.
Two morning doves resting on a wire,
carrying light to the city.

At the minute hand, we stand.
Two children in a celestial forest,
listening to the crackle of the branches.
Aware yet unafraid.

At the second hand, we run.
Two fireworks sent out over the lake,
bursting past time's ozone.
Scattered amber shards caress the water.

This watch is stitched to my wrist
with a rose stem.
When we stare at it, the thorns remind me that
we are all bound by the hands that
grip our necks and
pin us to the wall of germination.

My eyes are shut.
Eyelids, tattooed with the marrow of her soul.
The watch tightens,

so I look towards her for help.
I hold her palms and our fingers woven.
The thorns melt off my wrist, like newborn
snow into the grains of the desert sand.

**growth.**

You see the potential in me
that I thought I lost years ago.

## orion's fingertips.

Her heart faced the North Star.
"I feel so small."

He felt constellations on her palms.
Reflecting off her eyes, stars.
Galaxies wrapping around her shoulders.
Orion resting on her fingertips.

His heart, a telescope, focused on her.
"My night sky."

## rescind me.

I bought a casket for dying love.
Cherry oak.
The most expensive I could find.
I took my shovel and she took leave.
A one-sided love.
The coin had landed on my side.

I bought a casket for dying love.
Cherry oak.
To pay homage for such a young loved life.
My dying love for her,
now six feet below my feet.
The wildflowers sprung out through the dirt.
Roots attached to the wooden box.
Purple and meadow green buds opened.
Love cannot be stopped.
The tombstone reads, "Love cannot be rescinded."

**prayer.**

Look your neighbor or
a stranger or your mother in the eye.
Tell them each: you are more than
a bundle of reckless atoms, but rather an
offspring of Adam, gifted by God to me.

Push off and carry the bed sheets at sunrise to
cover the cold man on the corner store stoop.
Call your brother who works two connecting
flights away to remind him that distance is two
syllables just like "love you."

Show your teeth in smile song to the six-month-
old peering over his mother's sturdy shoulder.
Make faces so embarrassing, you can't bear
to look in the tinted mirror.

Giggles and smiles sent back. The mother has
no idea why but keeps the child tight.

No idea.

You look down as the mother turns to find out
the cause of her child's sudden joy.

You look down.
At your folded hands.

## **bound.**

he put on a ring.
a commitment ring.
a ring he was not going to take off.
for a while at least.
it was not for a girl
but for him.
to remind himself that he needed to change.
that he had work to do.
he would mess up.
as we all do.
but each time after
he would tap the ring
against a surface.
three times.
and to that beat.
he would say.

*faith.*

*faith.*

*faith.*

## one another.

I don't care if you know me or don't.
I don't care if you hate me, spit on me,
or wish I were dead.

When I see you I am going to love you.

I don't care if you don't believe me.
I don't care if I do not believe it myself.
I will.
And I will.
And I always will.

**it does not matter.**

It does not matter if I see the Tuscan hills.
The Grand Canyon.
Or the pyramids in Egypt.
When I see a stranger caring for another.
That is when I am breathless.
That is when I am pressed between
the bandage of humanity.

## pouring echoes.

I sat at the tip of the canyon.
Whispering my fears to the wind.
I sang out my joys, and asked
forgiveness for my sins.

An echo poured back at me. I listened
and heard everything I sought to be.
I heard my cries much sharper.
My joys doubled with laughter.
My uncertainty bold-faced.

I shimmied my feet, as I whistled on the ledge.
I walked my hands back to pull myself from the rock.
My fingers grasped onto a rope, a shoelace.
Peering up I saw 7 billion. All shouting
the same words forward, blind to the others to
their left and to their right.

The echo did not come from across
the canyon, but from behind.

I made it my mission to connect the hands
so that the 7 billion may feel the lines in the
palms of their neighbor.
That they may feel the hum of the voices
and realize the echoes aren't
from their heart alone but pouring from all.

## yes, it is.

It's not your problem.
You don't need to worry about me.
Yes it is.
When the man on the corner
can't afford a soup can,
That is my problem.

If the problem is in the world.
That is our problem.

## wheels don't step.

Whenever I see a crack on the sidewalk
I step on it.
To break my Mommy's back of course.

Last year in kindergarten when I
broke my pinky playing tag the
doctor said to me,
"It will grow back stronger now."

Mommy said the long lumpy pipe
on her back is not so strong anymore.
I think I have one too, but can't see it.

I can never see her bumpy back though.
It is always pressed against the seat
of her black chair with wheels.
I can't even see over the handles
Dad uses to push Mommy.

Mommy told me her lumps would
never get better.
But I'm not going to listen.
Her feet dangle
and the two metal wheels don't step
they just roll over the cracks.

That's why she isn't better yet.
So I do it for her.
Step on the cracks.
So one day she will wake up,
and be strong again.

During recess my friends and I
play on the broken driveway.
I told them what the doctor said.
I told them about Mommy.
We stepped together. On every crack.
And I know.
I know.
That Mommy will be well.

## machine world.

We can't look each other in the eyes
Because we are so fearful
That we will rediscover our humanity.

It is not our cracked screens that need fixing
but our shattered intentions.

I understand the struggle. I really do.

It is not that you do not want to rediscover
the love of your brother.
You just need a little help remembering.
Because TV stands for Tattered Vision.

I can assure you, if you connect your eyes
like puzzle pieces with your neighbor,
your vision will be sewn together
as well as the cuts the screen glass has left on
your hands.

**ten.**

If the average life expectancy is around 71 years.
That is 2,240,543,592 seconds.
That is 10 numbers.
Our phone numbers also have 10 numbers.

Don't let the 10 of your phone override
the 10 of your life.

## the weight of it all.

She looked out the window and she cried.
Not for what she had lost, but for what she had gained.

Weight.

And she did not care.
That old mirror was shattered.
Peering into each shard
her reflection unclouded.
Her tears triumphant.

Because.

They said don't stick your index finger
against the unmarred throat.
But she already loaded the gun
and with her finger pressed the

Trigger.

She did not see a weapon.
It was a magic wand to
make her beautiful.

Now.

The spoon and fork were no longer scalding.
She drank the milk from the hanging bag.
A newborn strengthened by the nursery.

She looked out the window and cried.
Not for what was lost, but what was gained.

Her index finger rest outside her jean pocket.
She noticed it. Gun barrel scarred
by the force of teeth.
However, the gun was more beautiful now.
A reminder that she had fought back.

The car came to a halt.
She was home now.
She looked out the window and
Did not cry.

## the pace.

the energy isn't swimming in the coffee cup.
it is in the people around you
in their tired feet and shaken hands.
walk at their pace
that is where the energy lives.

## x-ray vision.

We read x-rays.
But, the solution is not black and white.

Let us not forget
The words of the parents which become an
internal rocking chair.
The beads of sweat that paint the lands
of labor.
The anxiety of a lost twenty-dollar bill.

We read x-rays.
But the physician cannot tell
Where the patient has walked.

Look beyond the blackened snow.
See the forgotten ground.

## marked up.

Not only does the teacher have a red pen
But so do the students.
A pen used not for paper
But for the bodies of their classmates.
To circle what they find wrong.

They only write because they are afraid
That they are too red.

## thanks to give.

One day.
No.
Tomorrow.
I will wake up.
Finally thankful.
That my eyes kissed sunlight.

**carry.**

Everyone has baggage.
You just need to choose what you are willing to carry.

## linked.

I was born with a chain-linked fence
around my heart.
For every person I love a chain has been added.
For every love lost the chain is rattled.
I tried to rip the link, but I cannot
Because what was added cannot be taken away.

## empathy is the answer.

The telephone wire between two souls is
empathy.
Do not ever let the power go out.
Because once it does,
You will be left in the dark.

## be broken.

don't be a working vending machine
where people give to you, so you give to them.
be a broken vending machine.
the kind that spit out change from the bottom
for no reason.
be that.

## i will hold up your head.

If only I could cup the faces of every living
person. Direct their eyes towards mine.
Lock our gaze with a newborn key.

I would tell them that they matter to me.
I would tell them that their future matters to me.
I would tell them that the story of their past
matters to me.

They would try to look away.

They would think, "He must be a liar. What are
his intentions? What are his motives?"

But I would keep my hands steady and our eyes
locked.

Even when their tears would cause my hands to
slip.

I am not letting go.

Because when you believe in someone, you
cannot let go.

I would repeat again and again to them
What my beating heart believes.

*You matter to me.*

I would watch their pupils expand.
Attracted to the idea that they are not alone.
Finally, starting to believe that their feet
are pressing on the earth.
A tiny weight effecting its rotation.

## zipper in your chest.

There is a zipper woven in our hearts.
In the morning it is stuck.
We must make the choice.
To leave it knotted.
Or.
To use all of our courage. To rip it open.
And let the love go.

## sought.

What if.
You knew to be true.
That after a few years of trying.
You will accomplish whatever you sought to do.

**infinite…**

I don't believe in happy endings.
I believe in joy.
And joy does not have an end.

## you are not the driver.

bundle up your pride.
carry your vanity.
box up your greed.
harbor your doubt.
zip up your fear.
put it all in your moving truck.
and He will drive it away.

## peace and the cross.

you will know He hears your beating heart
when you can see the cross in the peace sign.

**write**

You must write the sentence
before you write the period

# About the Author

Nicholas John Bellacicco was born and raised in Stamford, CT. He attended Baylor University in Waco, TX. At Baylor he studied Medical Humanities and graduated with a Bachelor of Arts degree in University Scholars. He is passionate about the art dimension of medicine. He is currently in his first year of medical school at LECOM-Bradenton. He is first author of a journal paper on the importance of empathy in medicine. As well as poetry, Nick enjoys writing blog posts. Nick's blog can be found at wanderinginwondertoday.com.

**Disclaimer & Copyright Information**

The author and publisher have made every effort to ensure that the information in this book was correct at press time, the author and publisher do not assume and hereby disclaim any liability to any party for any loss, damage, or disruption caused by errors or omissions, whether such errors or omissions result from negligence, accident, or any other cause.

All content, unless otherwise noted,
is attributed to the Author.
Cover illustration and production

Copyright © 2017 by
Tribute Publishing, LLC
www.TributePublishing.com

www.ingramcontent.com/pod-product-compliance
Lightning Source LLC
Chambersburg PA
CBHW050536300426
44113CB00012B/2127